The Tin Book

To Lesley
with best wishes

Gordon Hoyles

26.08.2021

First published 1978

This edition published by Hardpressedbooks 2015

Cover design, Charlie Peacock ©

Back cover image: Neil Arnold

Front cover photograph Claire McNamee

ISBN: 10-1508919038
ISBN-13: 978-1508919032

DEDICATION

For Blossom

ACKNOWLEDGMENTS

I sincerely thank all of the people who have helped the success of The Tin Book by providing exhibition space on their establishments, and all those who have transported the tins to the places I could not personally reach.

Though too numerous to mention individually, to them all I am gratefully indebted.

G.W. Hoyles
April 1978

This Edition:
Blossom has steered this edition into print with enormous help and support from Anita and Charlie Peacock.

April 2015

ABOUT THIS EDITION

During the 1970's Gordon Hoyles' poetry output was prolific and his work breathtakingly honest as always. Enduring hardship, with no money for printing, he turned necessity into a virtue and wrote a poem on the white enamelled side taken from an old gas oven. Page One of 'The Tin Book' was born.

Other 'Tin pages' were created and exhibited around the towns and countryside of Hebden Bridge and further afield causing quite a stir.

'Soon there were tins in London and Liverpool and thickly clustered in many parts' and the Tins were regularly changed in each location in order to provide the public with a new poem to read, until the number 100 had been reached.

All 100 Tins were later exhibited together as a collection at The Precinct Centre Library, Oxford Street, Manchester, in February 1979.

We thought that this extraordinary collection should be seen again by a modern audience in a different context. The poems reflect the life and times of Gordon and Blossom Hoyles at Bell House Farm in the mid '70's and were a stepping stone towards Gordon's development as a performance poet in the 1980's.

We have tried to remain faithful to the original paperback publication and hope that we have managed to retain some of the energy, enthusiasm and ingenuity with which they were first created.

Hardpressedbooks

The story of the first edition is told in Gordon Hoyles' inimitable style from page 111 of this edition.

These poems have all retained

the ‘page numbers’ of the original **Tins**

Page One

Drawings Chris Cullen

There was a country bumpkin
    Who thought he'd reach the sky
So he tried for several weeks
    To make a saddle for a fly.

Then he walked a country lane
    to the top of yonder hill
And there he sat quite puzzled
    'cos he couldn't reach it still.

He began to build a staircase
Up which he'd surely get
But he climbed into a cloud
And came down wringing wet.

This made him feel so weary
He went straight home to bed
And his snoring came as
Thunder from his head.

Page Two

The fire gives the boiler
    a very hot seat
Steam hurrying off
    escapes the heat.

It goes to a cylinder
    down a pipe.
The piston not standing
    sighs a wipe.

Under the strain the
    crosshead helps the crank,
And for all this upset
    wonders who to thank.

While the wheel so excited
    does a turn
And a thousand tons
    follow their stern.

As the whole sniffs and chunters
    swinging on the rails
The whistle joins the chorus
    with wooing wails.

So the steam joins
    the smoke to look at the stir
And flies a freedom streamer
    fluffy in the air.

Page Three

A kangaroo of a hullabaloo
It's giblets simply grew and grew
A plate of plum and custard too
All of a fluster of dobbley brew.

Page Four

And in the beginning was the word. And there came the conjunction and the word begat a word that begat a word till there was a book. And nouns mattered and verbs and adjectives. And sitting in rooms reading, the reading book begat a book which begat a book which begat a book which begat a book which begat a book and reading books are breeding reading books and profusion has brought confusion as message meaning is obscured. Nouns are still. But the adjective has become everything as waiting they watch someone else translate the hard verbs.

They spend themselves on small fights and many are pointing the way shouting help whilst protecting the problems against solution.

Page Five

Brilliant

vivid flash   Poetree

Dazzling

Could soldier nits in read the Windscale weather

forecast on radio activity.

Page Six

Looking into the Maze

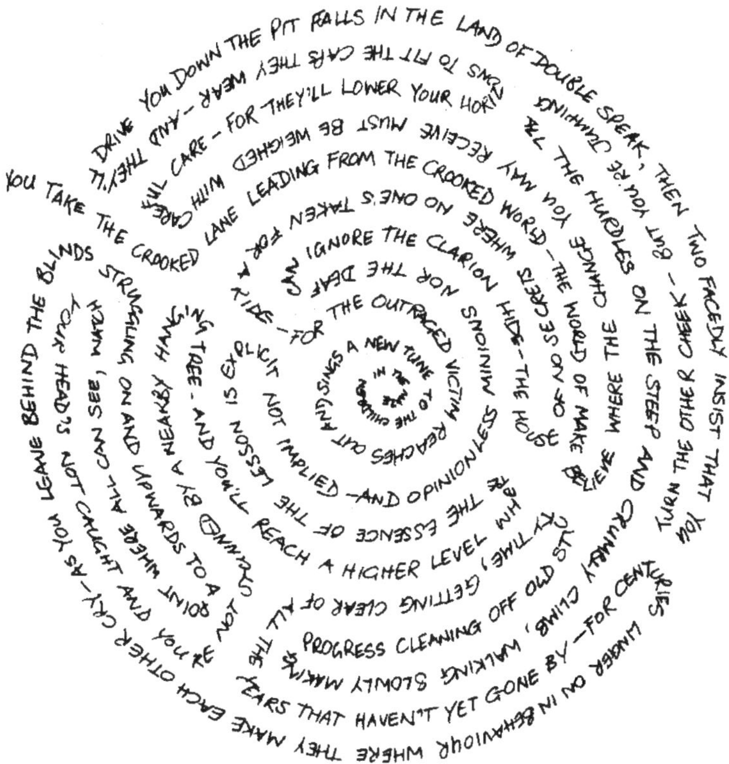

Page Seven

Gwoiley made an oil can
With which to oil the mice
He didn't like their squeaking
Otherwise he thought them nice.
Yap! go the mouse traps
Lashing empty air.
Eat all the cheese up
Sample without care.

Page Eight

Stoodley Pike

Mighty mast symbolic steeple
Towers aloof the scoundrel pound,
dwarf dwellings and misplaced power
that reign a psychopathic hour
And gain a conquest over what?

Rightly cast away from people,
fast cut and thrust and stupid cash,
above the brutal maniac past.

That better, good and peace might last
here was cut a prayer in rock.

Page Nine

Hebden Bridge

Nestling in a difficulty
      rent in England's earth
Need provoked a settlement
      endurance proved its worth.

Angular steep and craggy
      dwellings stand the tilt
Linked by tangled track
      stack on stack and solid built.

Step by step struggling's record,
      sculpted living grit
As grim determination makes
      the best a better bit.

Page Ten

Now z had the feeling of being pushed off the end, so had a word with y. Y passed the complaint to x who phoned v. V got in touch with u who went to t with s, who being a bit twisted wrote to r in a month, whilst waiting the q was p. O said n was annoyed that m was told first, L was glad to hear about the problem and thought it would be a good thing to be rid of some of the less active members. Provoked, k and j convened a conference with h, issuing a joint statement which said g. When I laughed, f said e would advise d, who, because c isn't straight, said he'd find out what b had to say. Finally the message got through to a .

'A' proceeds to tell everyone including z, that he knew about the situation all along, but didn't move. And that left z as before but more flummoxed, flabbergasted, frustrated and utterly powerless.

Page Eleven

Going on record depending on notice,
Working in letters lovely intentioned assiduous man,
Hopefully offers you language experience sharing.

Page Twelve

The souvenir monger
    humdrums merrily along
applying trimmings liberally
    he sings a ditty song.

I'll do one if you please sir,
    to commemorate the day.
You'll cherish what I do sir,
    I'll cherish what you pay.
Would you like a stick of rock, sir,
    or something made of clay.
I've the very thing in stock ,sir,
    it's a plate of take away.

Page Thirteen

Going on regardless day or night
Wishes insisting loom large in ample minds.
Holding one your living's exciting surprise.

Page Fourteen

Trickery bickery flock
much that's about is mock
they knock on and on
they're silly and wrong
bickery trickery stop

Page Fifteen

Getting up when it pleases,
Wholly independent, unafraid,
He has upper crust for breakfast
Only drinks best accolade
Yokles here and there all around
Long laughing shakes the still
"'e wants it on a plate, "
Says old goodie Blunder Bill.

Page Sixteen

They eat daily pretend bread
coated with a sham jam spread,
in scenery especially canned
clean and nice and second hand.
That is, everybody ‘cept Seamus.

With news bespoke tailor made
for children by the media trade,
all stand behind a shiny front
keyed up, ready, eager to stunt.
That is, everybody, ‘ cept Seamus.

Page Seventeen

Don’t twist yourself.

    To solve the riddle,

ask who’s got

    the biggest diddle.

Page Eighteen

Now I'm a little rodent,
And I'm somewhat like a mole,
I live beneath the bracken
Up a lovely little hole

At the top of the valley
Where white mountains meet,
And it's entrance, silky smooth,
Is a gently sloping treat.

It's snug and warm and cosy
Just below the water spout
And when there's no-one looking
I go skidding in and out.

Sometimes nibbling in my mouth
The very sweetest honey.
I bet a rodent my type's
As good as being a bunny.

For I jump and frisk about
Till I'm all over come,
Then I settle satisfied
Well pleased with what I've done.

And happy after playing
I go floppy off to sleep.
Never do I rack my brain
With things like counting sheep.

Page Nineteen

I know a funny man
    and a crow lives up his nose.
I heard he grows potatoes
    in his socks between his toes.

I've seen carrots in his ears,
    but I don't know why he chose
To carry his allotment
    everywhere he goes.

Page Twenty

Playing with materials in
never end pretend. Driven
to acquire the envy of a
friend.

The see-through house and
hustle bustle of the children
in the playground has gone
nowhere and found nothing.
They compete and fight and
jostle for admiration
consoled moments and suddenly
the whistle blows.

Page Twenty One

Cannikins, manikins
    tremble and shake.
Manikins, cannikin
    make an earth quake?
Cannikin, manikins
    Amchitka boo!
Manikins cannikin
    make good with glue?

Manikins cannikin
    break up the earth?
Cannikin, manikin
    blast all your worth.
Manikins, cannikin,
    Amchitka boom!
Cannikin, manikins
    looking for doom?

Amchitka Island, Alaska, site of the largest nuclear bomb test in American history, code named Cannikin. The bomb of 5 megatons exploded at 11.00am on November 6th 1971

Page Twenty Two

It’s a scandal
Do not strangle
On a dangle
Try an angle

Turn the handle
Of the mangle.
Do not wrangle,
Work a wangle.

Says a vandal
To the jangle
Of his tangle
With a bangle

Page Twenty Three

I reside with sheep and shepherds
    in a state of dire want,
Which makes me try the harder
    and unbending stand.
As I slowly climb the hills
    I know I'm somewhere in the plan
Or else, I dare to say,
    there would be no such man.

YAA though I walk the valleys
    wearing rags and holey shoes
And now and then carouse
    and join with others on the booze,
I fear none;
For I plod the path, art with me,
    square and straight and true.

I go forth quite determined
    these values will succeed.
If they're allowed to fail,
    we are less than what we need.
In which case, let us gladly
    toll the final knell,
For this world is forever
    inconsequential hell.

Page Twenty Four

Spitting, sitting down lolloping hobble
labour set bones, black spotted fly
blown crusty scones, grunting grumbling
tones telling what they've done ten
fold as big, doing what they did ten
fold the shortest way putting miles
and miles in a single bale of hay.

How many cows make a fat pig? How
many dogs bark in a a pair of clogs?
Forefathers make rods for their backs.
Parents twisted by their forebears, drunk
on the parental spring inherit and
inheriting pass on the cup. Slavering
and lathering stupidly bent, they won't
grow.

There's berries on the bushes, apples
on the trees and fishes in the stream.
The apiary's on overtime because of
all the bees and the sun's up in Heaven.

Page Twenty Five

Though his multi coloured tatters
    make a poor weather shield,
He sports a knitted titfer
    on his great big tousled head.
Is he doing much that matters
    in the middle of the field?
For he doesn't seem to work
    yet, what does he do instead?

As a king upon a throne
    he surveys the evergreen,
With the wind blowing through him,
    he's that thin and under-fed.
Whilst he clearly stands alone
    has he embarked on pure dream?
Which brings one further question:
    Does a scarecrow go to bed?

Page Twenty Six

Calm green see rotary zeewergee
round and round mechanical racket
and tractor gas riding the grass
knocks it down to stubs and
stripes.

The sun's baking, hay making
crinkle-crankle froffy buff.

Centipede scatters fluffy hay
makes froffy see.

Wuffler wuffles up buff rollers.

Mechanical racket and tractor gas,
clickaty dunk clickaty dunk
into big MacCormick chunk.

Clickaty dunk, clickaty dunk,
hurry up hurry up tractor gas,
hurry up sound, mechanical pounding
clatterings natterings finding
the mind. Hurry up hurry yup
clickaty dunk clickaty dunk
clickaty dunk clickaty dunk clickaty dunk
clickaty dunk clickaty dunk upaty
dunk tractor gas.

The scrape of the stone, the sigh
of the scythe, the fork and the rake,
man sized for man's sake make time
to take it in.

The perfumed air, the whispering
crisp, tea drinking, voices speaking
assimilating, mutual feeling.

Page Twenty Seven

Genius operates rashly discounting outraged normals.
Whereas, inspiration's lightning lashes it's anointed man,
Having opted, yearns to linger even spread.

Page Twenty Eight

Wonderful man he was.
Investigating each because,
Lifting every standard higher
Leaving nothing to desire.
Imprisoned for his fortitude.
Administration wanting rectitude.
Master of his destiny
He leapt above the common rank.
Outsize fish in this small tank.
Looking deep at every sample
This man set the best example.

Page Twenty Nine

Whilst "Under a Japanese Parasol"
Incessantly seeking the road
Leading all the unexplored,
Lone one of a kind he carried his load
Incensed by the need to go on.

As dedicated hypocrites called him odd,
Matchless intelligence asserted itself.
He laboured for others, long on his tod
Outside the pitiful realm of self.
Learning with detailed precision
This man made a fool of derision.

An acrostic on the name ***William Holt*** *who wrote 'Under a Japanese Parasol'*

Page Thirty

Friends of friends vainly smiling
pleasant as a surface scum,
hiding little nonsense secrets
guarding closely mischief done.

Top nobs riding in low gear
on the nerve racked intrigue run
It's no surprise the social circle
gets nowhere and little's won.

Page Thirty One

For not telling lies she was thought unwise
and would surely come a cropper
Though told and told and told again
not nobody could stop her.

So,

For Topsy Turvy always unwary
they made a special down fall
"It only serves her right,"
proudly shouted each and all.

But,

She smiled and smiled thereafter
finding gravity a treat,
For she landed safe and up right,
squarely on her feet.

Page Thirty Two

Mummy mummy, ugly farmer George is
playing with his swastika and the
colonies are fighting for their
basic rights, life, liberty and the
pursuit of happiness.

Mummy , why has ugly farmer George
got such a big fat tummy he does no
proper work and we work all the time
and we're thin and hungry?

Admiral Nelson says us people live
in shocking conditions and we
shouldn't have to. Mummy why isn't
Admiral Nelson, King, why mummy why?

Shush little David, you shouldn't
say that, fat ugly farmer George
wouldn't like it. Remember fat ugly
farmer George and his henchmen hung
your daddy.

And they hung Uncle Thomas too,
because he was helping hungry people.
Why mummy, why? It's not good mummy,
it's not good. The land is black
with hanging people.

Shush, little David, Shussh. Fat
ugly farmer George might get you.

Page Thirty Three

Anti decline stuggles uphill

Dragging the dregs, the vicious
loathesome underhill samaritans.
Hopeless cases, podge faced,
obese, faithless conceited clay,
trembling inferior trash.
Wasters, gold plated parasites,
terrified liars rolling no where.
Powerful sick, bad garbage.

Page Thirty Four

Pretending for whose benefit?
The poor earth can't stand it
and they dare not look.
It's not just a joke. This is.

Everything in the garden should
be coming up cabbages. But the
idiots, shy and unhappy in the
make up watch the roses flower and die.

Page Thirty Five

Mouth to ears to mouth to ears
Tell all the world in thirty years.

But silent eyes pages scan
and quick as light message can
penetrate the whole of man.

Page Thirty Six

Tenderly the weaver and the wizard
Raddle roved the cobbled stair.
Inclosed in alleyways of hopeless despair.
Gripping substance out of pipe dream,
Gracefully the mystic conjured fable
Easing from the base mix magic stable.
Reality and fantasy inseparably embrace.

Page Thirty Seven

Turned loose, shaft free,
Running overjoyed
In response to the horn.
Grazing fondly,
Galumph adventurer,
Enchanted beast,
Ridden by his lover.

Page Thirty Eight

Perfection needs no hard sell
and has no anti climax
needing lazy fat hindsight analysis.
With my life I fight towards the boundary.

Page Thirty Nine

When minds yield the field expands
    before the rocking horse
And mounting brings horizons
    to a central bobbing point
As through the tender coupling
    flows the pleasure force.

Then frantic fast the charge
    propelled on loosened reins
As all the motion doth with joy anoint
So sweet's the life when comings
    take away the strain
And known's the peace
    that is our greatest glory
For all the journeyings taught
    there is no journey
Thus is all travellers tale
    a shaggy horse story.

Page Forty

The bystanders tight-lipped watch the
confrontation build up. Predictions,
preparations based on assumptions.
all are waiting, the whole reliant upon
the unknown quantity.
Enchanted beast,
Years, months, weeks, days, hours,
minutes, seconds———ignore. Comprehend
the moment. The moment is most critical.

Page Forty One

Nearly two thousand years and all the inns
are still full.

The papers passing round the churning systems
ridicule the essence as the pressure of the clamp
down squeezes through the routine.

When the spirit's killed.   Will there be
churning churning churning with no peaks
until wanting climax turns horrendous to turn
on.

Page Forty Two

Over-acting minor parts the deluded
swagger rasping conceits and agog
the kiddies swallow whole unhealthy
deceits.

All are bewildered by oppression till
the flimsy breaks and the substance shows
as the cracking shrieks wilder fabrications,
crude and threatening.

But the drunken know the facts they face
disgrace them.

Page Forty Three

Type

Daughters were educated by their mothers who screwed their fathers grew up to be battered wives, the raw material of a new fast expanding no growth energy disperser business.

Page Forty Four

Sons pained in training to provide
secure ease for their parents in their
dotage, resent, rebel and retaliate as
sensibility surfaces and become
wife-batterers. during the withdrawal process.

Page Forty Five

Question: "Tell me. Where are we going?"

Answer: " Why are we going there?"

Page Forty Six

The big fat kid
is as thick as a tank,
His daddy died laughing
with cash in the bank.

He willed him nothing
just left him slogging
And the glutton kid
keeps on flogging.

Since his daddy died
he does his own thrashing,
Thinks self flagellation
is double smashing.

As acute paranoia
the psychopath rears
The Bunterly fool
kills none of his fears.

Page Forty Seven

Warning.

Pole ease tate pending.

Not a pea sea!
    special landscapist!
    dective!
    mife a gent?????

Danger!   danger!   danger!

Rally now.

Page Forty Eight

Denied, bullied, badgered, taunted, harassed,
crushed by fluxial forces he lays hidden
believing he can't reach, as he's forbidden.

Ambivalence, ever ready, beats the barriers
as rousing images swell. He jumps the breach
and blows care away breathing defiance.
Serene the quick release, unassailable the peace
of Master Bating's tale of victory and triumph.

Page Forty Nine

Just ice creams at the rule ——————

the law, cold and partial, stiff and raw ———-

the truncheon tool, the disqualifier.

Our tongues as our minds lick and lap

and move as our understanding, emotions,

spirits.

Let our tongues lick and whip the cold

and raw truncheon tool, just ice creams.

Page Fifty

If you've a job
to stop your gob
stick your tongue out
let it lolly

If it's nagging
if it's braggin'
stop it waggin'
let it lolly

Hold your noise
know speechless joys
and invest
for best interest
in authentic knowledge
stick your tongue out
lick a lolly
cool and jolly good
it's understood

Know what you're doin'.
Keep your mouth shut chewin'

Page Fifty One

Little smudges clinging to their
fabrication, jellies in their
structures all solids left by smudges.

And always closest to them unrevealed
the smudge is pushed further to
the background throwing up the
forms in the cross ply adventure
playground set ups where each seeks
their smudge and as none come
clean going through the motions
postpone the smudge discovery
till polished dotting I's weep
alone for their smudge is
as unknown and in no smoothie
group does the interface and
smudge embrace so much
feign yet all contain the
secret smudge space the key
to understanding.

Page Fifty Two

What do you think of the world situation?

We're somewhere opposite the moon.

Page Fifty Three

And now you know of all there is
        and know it isn't much
That differences are minor
        and change is subtle touch

Universal is the core,
        unalterable the soul,
Blending first and last
        in homogenous whole.

Page Fifty Four

Before you attack this simple stand
    reflect on the plans you've made in vain
And think of the ones who've loved me.

As the hour glass weeps our grains of sand,
    think of the ones who love you.

Page Fifty Five

The famous thing.

Enters private thought and loud debate,
Enduring hangs about persistent as a wait.

Is known to those who won't admit they know
and won't believe the certainty they saw:

The blinkered and blinkered indifferent
That nothing group the deliberate ignorant

By all the anti's and the for's
and ever present care less scores.

Is with all who know they share
In everything and everywhere

And those who're apt to get annoyed
with equalness they can't avoid.

For each is needed to begin
and truly make the famous thing.

As seen by millions off television.

Page Fifty Six

One , two three four
I believe there's several more.
A B C D
what's it got to do with me?
Jack, Queen, King, Ace
I am in the human race.

Page Fifty Seven

Hopefully the blinkered eyes discover cells
of planted pain releasing locks that intrigue
set then threw away the key.

Allow yourself the tolerance to see, to
over-ride those constraints the mechanics
of fear so deftly applied, and feel the
welcome warmth and inner warm when blinkers
are no longer worn.

Page Fifty Eight

Committee is a party game,
it's meetings social do
Where round and round the parrot planes
and sometimes back and to.

When at last the bird's quite plucked
the eating's oft deferred
Because of flattery flutterings
which needn't have been heard.

Page Fifty Nine

Please allow your eyes to see

and let your ears hear

For you're allowed to disbelieve

whatever may appear.

Page Sixty

A day break stroll about the hamlet
open cast my mind
Just enjoying the imbibing
of what is to find.

I head towards the shopping centre's
studied neat arranged inside:
Watch the river's hurried running
sago pudding ride.

Then a bird's trill song surprises
reaching through the clear air,
Trim, new trees and fresh laid paving,
old and modern. Everywhere
Spick and brushed and freshly tidied.

How delightful, fine and balanced
politicians set the stage.

So, as a badger which has sensed the dawn,
I scurry into the alleyway and enter my
secluded new residence. There I rest,
pensive sullen. In a little while I hear
the charging dinosaurs go snorting by
in search of open pasture.

Page Sixty One

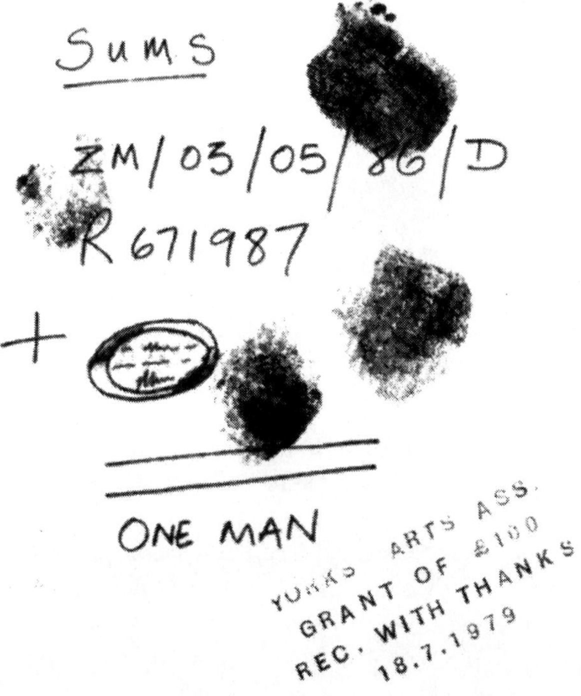

Page Sixty Two

What they cannot budge though they penetrate
    they won't perpetrate on more
And at once and in each and all things and all ways
    they're constantly seeing the flaw.
But they cannot expand for the air is so crammed
    with nonsensical heart-breaking jaw,
O how many poets have jumped at the chance
    to get themselves killed in a war?

Page Sixty Three

Dear God,
I hope you are well.
I keep praying, but I suppose
you get a lot of that. Who
wants what must take some
unscrambling. It's an absolute
mystery how you work. I'm
not complaining but I don't
seem to be getting through,
so I thought I'd drop you a
line. For Christ's sake
you gave me a load. I'm
grateful you gave me what I've
got, and a lot of it and good
quality. I'm using it all, but,
~~ and I'm not making excuses
~~ it's the jamming, the
jamming down here's hellish.
I don't seem to be getting
through and I thought you
ought to know. There's just
one thing I'm wanting now,
and that's a proper good
result. Anyway God,
that's all for now. Be seeing
you. Thanking you in
anticipation,

Yours faithfully

Page SixtyFour

Disco

Pee zumpee zumpee zoo
Pee zumpee zumpee zoo
Pee zumpee zumpee zoo
I love you

Pee zumpee zumpee zoo
Pee zumpee zumpee zoo
Pee zumpee zumpee zoo
I need to.

Page Sixty Five

If you're bending towards

what you haven't chose

It's the musical

breaking pianos

Page Sixty Six

Aware, sensitive, watchfully alert they hurriedly work.   Peeping, seeing, ragged daubed with dirt urchins survive the sleek and sneaking shifty vermin cloaked in grey and live until they die.

Page Sixty Seven

I’m walking home. Down and far away
behind the town shows it’s fixed flames,
the embers of a spent day.
Did it matter anyway,
the ordinary importance play

That stuck a pin in Jimmy’s mouth,
Sent Douglas Demon cycling south,
After it had beat down Jean,
Thrown spanners in Freddie’s dream
And put a check on little Sue.

All chattering, the lemmings flew.

Page Sixty Eight

There’s a thing about
    called the wonder bug
Which feeds upon the
    honey shrub.
It doesn't fly
    nor creep nor jump
Somehow it pours.
    I wouldn’t say it’s plump.
It’s call is a
    singing to the lugs
And any who it bites
    come up in sugar lumps.
They’re very hard to find,
    where they live I couldn’t say,
Happen you’ll meet one
    on your lucky day.

Page Sixty Nine

Friddly middley upsaddy ho
Inkery dreamery way wo
Clutching the flux in the haze of the day
Singery crackally singally play
Scraping and picking and blowing a go
Heavery mingery dooly a bo

Page Seventy

I'll tell you the tale
    of hairy Bill
Who lives with
    little Daffodil

As little boy playing
    thought what's to be done?
He tried snakes and ladders
    the other lad won.

And he wasn't found
    when they played hide and seek.
So he stayed hidden
    for nearly a week.

Whilst he was wondering
    where he'd gone wrong,
He blew his tin trumpet
    mellow and strong.

Page Seventy One

Audacity.

It may seem a mite absurd to
mint another household word
like door mat,
dog, acrobat,
Billy Bunter, Dr. Who,
Andrews, a dose of flu,

Vinegar, salt, chips and fish

A good old fashioned seasonal wish.

Page Seventy Two

The in genius,
proceeding without plan
from safe as always.
Extremist in the van
playing checkers
taking others where they never thought of going
and giving them good reason.
Phenomenal benign force
seeming like an emotional disturbance.
Effort to somewhere
knows only the goal.
Strange is LEADERSHIP

Page Seventy Three

much that is paenstaekingli taut
for proegres must bee unlernd
and teediusli the snael
leevs a shieni silver trael

as the peddlers ov gimmick
deefend the fortuens ernd.
the clangers driev coffin naels
in iriversabl saels.

Page Seventy Four

We can depend upon the bees
to make the honey
And the spider can be left
to make a web,
It's other folk that cause
the bother being funny.

Page Seventy Five

There's a cottage by a traffic stream
    that no-one should ignore
It has decibelic diesel
    stereo-piped to every floor.

And none could fail to pick up
    the articulate vibes
Which are felt from top to bottom
    and are known to shake the sides.

In its garden growing
    there's health foods by the bed
Veg that's radiation proof
    foliage fed the purest lead.

In every way a residence
    ideal for a slave
For unless compelled to live there
    who could summon so much brave?

Page Seventy Six

Again a sunrise, again a day
Again the children learn and play
the customary thing, the usual way.

All is familiar.   Yet all is new.
There'll be no repeat of time, nor repeat of you.
Just a future in common to contribute to.

Page Seventy Seven

Alternative.

On the level, why go uphill?
"The problem."
Scrap it.
"Need."
Use it up.
"Heat."
Like it.
"Light."
The dark's so restful.
"Food."
It grows on trees.
"Work."
Relax. Give it to the machines.
"I'm not sure."
Conserve energy, do less.
"Convince me.?"
Living on easy street's effortless.
"What will we do?"
Be content.

Page Seventy Eight

Taking a thought wrench to the bogus
Stimulates emotional outbursts.

When the relief valve stops hissing
        and re-seats,
In the calm, reflections see and learning
moves towards new level equilibrium.

Page Seventy Nine

Once it's triggered reasons rifled
as in an instant, from a trifle
talk starts shouting
blurting shocking crazy quips,
sapping strength, distorting lips,
warping to destruction.
Forgetful of consequence
blacking out common sense
every impulse unrestrained
at domination injury's aimed
as spiked tangents run riot
in uncontrolled unquiet.
The tempest blasting
Blowing tissue stretching credence

Blurring focus mindlessness amuck

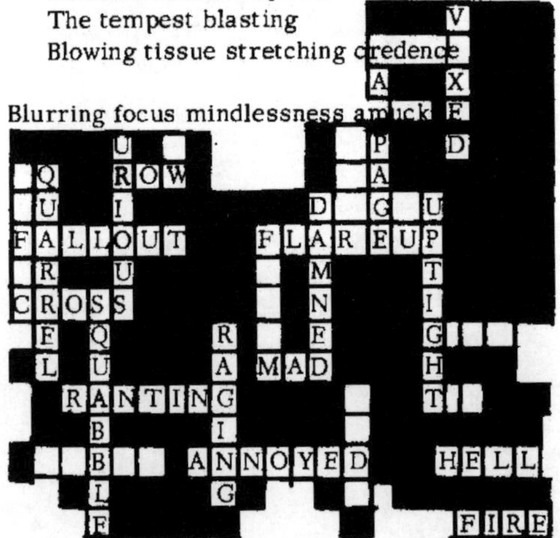

Page Eighty

Recipe for humble pie.

Take a trier, watch the trial,
then try the trier again.
If it comes up smiling,
then try the trier again.
When it's screaming like a lobster,
give more of the same.
Beat it, pound at, laugh at
the spectacle of pain.

Exercise all patience
as you force the breaking strain.
Then shrug and put the heat on
to cool it's claim.
Then pour in your solution
as you gently wash the brain.
Then watch it touch the bottom,
then put it down the drain.

Page Eighty One

If you turn to 8 till 4
and have no idea what for,
Please! don't fight me—- - - fight them!

If your stint is 9 to 5
and you feel but half alive,
Please! don't fight me—- - -fight them!

If you're treated like a tool
and the job you're on's a fool,
Please! don't fight me—- - -fight them!

If you're wriggling all around
as a worm below the ground,
Please! don't fight me—- - - fight them!

If you don't seem worthwhile
and you'd like a change of style,
Please! don't fight me—- - - fight them!

Page Eighty Two

1st Division:

Victims United v The Rest

Well, as was expected, starting with dirty dribbling it was foul play all the way. Pandemonium broke out when Victims United scored first from a corner and then off a penalty. This was too much for the Rest's right wing who killed their own goalie on the spot, hanging him from his own crossbar. Their fans went hysterical, frantically working their rackets they chanted,

"Hang him again! Hang him again!"

Whilst the Victims crowd rolled in the terraces laughing.

There followed the fanciest ever footwork. The ball was soon nowhere to be seen and long before half time they kicked each other to death.

Page Eighty Three

System's rejects surpass
the passers. The unperforated sheet
that passed the scanners
makes an unholy fortune.
Delighted stamp collectors know.

Page Eighty Four

Glad, happy clad patchwork
jumble sale misfits
constructively register dissatisfaction.
Quietly beckoning brightly,
charmingly interesting others in mending their
ways.

The gentle new culture,
a colourful classless cohesion,
preferring the home made, employs itself wholly;
participating enjoying pleasures and fun
with self-imposed leisurely discipline,
lifting the standard, restless until the job's
done to perfection.

Page Eighty Five

The Opposition

Non members, knots in the fretwork,
uncommitted empties oppose unaffected by
the outcome. Shining examples,
components of attention
vaguely groping for argument
sounding clever in service of vanity.
Power plays teasing vectors contradict, side
track, double back, eight track, happy crack,
joke and mock and make a nonsense.
Wiggle a bit.
Giggle a bit, ridicule, comic compare,
It's like. It's like a tike, a motor bike.

Jolly jolly followers catch a phrase,
Second phase, try to match the punch line.
Find the catch, mark time, interrupt, chime
in, raise a laugh interject some meaningless.
Stick a tag, be a wag;
It isn't just a brain storm,
she wants it all organically grown.

And Ignoratio Elenchi, victorious in stereo,
took over and didn't know what to do with
the winnings.

Page Eighty Six

Success kills them,
        or they die of failure.
Ambitions are cats that
        get squashed in the road.

Page Eighty Seven

A lot of people are fully occupied being unemployed.

And of course there are the under-employed trying to appear importantly busy.

The truth is most people in jobs need work.

What is work?

W, O, R, K, W is for worthwhile, O is for operations, R is for receiving, K is for kinaesthetics, Worthwhile operations receiving kinaesthetics.
Work.

There's not much of that going on.

They won't let things be that way.

What is the answer?

Destroy the working class.

Page Eighty Eight

Mild and gentle, busy, in the background
        debates the fuhrer touch
Supposing we're but play things
        and life is nothing much.
Though couched in simply homely terms
        she spins the old old lies
Whilst looking for the master key
        to be sure of winning a prize.
Though donkeys may heed the carrot con
        hollowly echoing worn propaganda gong

For your imagery's the tyranny
        planned to prolong the dark
As by using tricks backed by trumps
        dictators rise and bark.
Then the rest jump at the whim of one will
        and punished's all contrariness.
By what quirk could hearts be trumps
            When always trumps are heartless?

Page Eighty Nine

Scatter brained.

Get spaced out, buy the world.
Po knolly po brolly go mo mo
The wind sows the thistle and will sow the oat
as surely as the cradle crescent grows.
Kindness begs to be tested.
Machines mashing.
Some amuse themselves keeping secrets.
Each little bit is forced to fit
                    till all the picture's done
And every special features's been corrupted,
                    compromised away.
Puggally puggally wooger
Puggally puggally through
Ramstam.
Wanted: A woman for Robin. Needs to be
                    just average beautiful like us all.

Page Ninety

The system doesn't care for talk
Reason won't be heard when spoke.
Why confront the arbitrary divides?
Taking hammer and tongues to mind blocked
prejudice is a mugs game.
Mugs waste time arguing with the sub human
and their imaginary obstacles suffering inner
personal conflict as a consequence.

But as the system (the sub human phoney),
pays wages, the system is thought to be real.

Challenge the zodiac
One bland grand attack
We are, we are and we'll be.

Re-write the almanac
Making a better pack
We are, we are and we'll be.

It is true there is a sun warmed beach, lazy boats
and all round peace to which the road outside
has reach.

Page Ninety One

All we have on our side is what nature has provided
and nowhere in the universe can be found equality.

But on suzaphone
        and wee tin whistle
full note and demi semi quaver
        enter the discussion
putting something
        to the quality
of balanced repercussion.

Each flower and leaf
        and shade of colour
adding flavour to the score.

Carefully maintaining equilibrium, within the
boundless possibilities of unhampered inequality we live.

Page Ninety Two

Were I but a rich man,
        knowing all my worrying was done,

I would start a different circus
Every act the very best intent
All things just well used
        and nothing spent.

I'd buy a new bull dozer
        specially chosen
Just so I could doze the bull
There would be no moment left unfull.

We'd have healthy earth
and there'd be no battles
        to be won.

O God, I'm doing all I can,
Is it wrong to play an honest hand
and to be a wealthy man.

I'd guarantee to work hard
doing all the things we all
        of us want done
Finishing what ever was begun.

Page Ninety Three

Tra la lum die die die doe die,
Tra la lum die doe die day

The poor, tired of waiting timidly venture
from their hideouts intimidated by stains.
Hunted escapees rummaging, sifting the spin
off dodging about on the run with non-existent
papers. Nervous strain ready with awkward
lie. Fighting exhaustion,

Doe de dum die doe die doe die
Doe de dum die doe die day

Page Ninety Four

An apology to Donald Nielson.

As heartlessly raped is
willing labour
Through years and years
they set up the game
Withholding reward to
virtuous endeavour.
As evil rears evil
in some made clever
With ease the arch devil
assumes a new name.

A stealthy excitement shifts
as suddenly it's on,
And a shocking hell
tremours the ganglion.

Innocent dogs pant gulped
quickened breath
Demanding protection
and swift reprisals
And hope they're not next
to meet gruesome death.

Then there's stage managed
total denials
And closed's the show
with the star in a cage.
Thus extremes meet
with equivalent outrage.

Page Ninety Five

Cavorting with the specimens, magazine face
Caught in momentary vertical chase
Vortex to vortex, next to next.
Rapidly images fuse and blurr
As the smouldering pot is as it were.
So where is it getting us, getting us all?

When the blow's over, the artificial's burst
Awakening a little better than worst
The unpopular view's all that's new.
As old direction alters course
Reminiscing wards off remorse,
But where is it getting us, getting us all?

Page Ninety Six

Looking in every mirror for a nice reflection
to identify with.
Do, do and do,
to be as good as who?

Troubled, used admirers tumble into left behind
in the quest for entry to top bracket set-ups.

But the status givers have gone out of business
due to shortage of desirable prizes. So nobody's
watching as donning old habits the biped grimly
stays on the worn thin established track, but
the floating co-ordinates with years of experience
analyse and answer back.

Page Ninety Seven

Brush by sides seem velveteen
On the variable speed switch back glide
Where wild life flutters, flushed by the ride.
Luxury deep's the dark surround
And the way's all clear of indecision.
Not much can escape the narrow beam vision
Driving through the Trough at night.

Page Ninety Eight

Up Cragg Vale.

Cranny full of solids and soft, thrusting,
meeting high the narrow firmamental loft.
Exuding from its sides the living ooze
which joins the bottom gulley bed
        and smoothly tremoring woos.

In love the whole rejoicing
        blooms and wanes
As nature's intercourse replenishing
        itself, sustains.

Page Ninety Nine

It's fifteen degrees below
The peas in the soup are snugly buoyed up
by the dense and the lazy lie.
Starving, throwing acid, frying ice, I have told you,
told you all of the lazy lie.
You dirty filthy Christ killing scum. You foul the
earth you walk on.

Page One Hundred

With no weapon but appeal
it is not fit that I be still
And watch recurring evil
suffocate and kill.

Nor can I stay to see the
tortured children die
And walk amongst survivors
who've forgotten how to cry.

As if new born with
full developed mind
I must have challenge
of another kind
And learn as does a baby
finds it's tongue
Mimicking the sounds
until I've sentence sung.

About the Title

Cinderfella was sitting, wellingtoned feet in the ashes of the big fireplace in the draughty, comfortless kitchen musing deeply on the ways of his ugly brothers and talking a steady stream of thoughts to his beloved Princess Sticky, his only true companion.

He spoke for some time examining and considering, recalling meetings, actions, journeys, methods and motives, recapturing briefly the paths trod, feeling again the uplift of hopes entertained and re-living the let downs, the element of not quite which seemed to haunt them. Strange indeed that his ugly brothers thrived whilst clearly he and Princess Sticky could not acquire the bare necessities let alone simple extra little delights.

Drifting on this gist it suddenly occurred to him that

those who knew his poetry were a circle of intimates, a tight knot who, contrary to his good-natured belief that they were actively promoting his work, were effectively keeping him in check.

"My other cheek is getting sore," was his concluding lament. But without pause to draw breath he went on, "I will not yield. We must continue our goings about."

"The trouble is I get fed up with repeating myself, explaining who I am and what my business is whenever we visit a new place. I need a card," he said.

"We have no money for printing," said Princess Sticky sadly.

"Cards are not much good anyway. They get filed away, forgotten, soon thrown out. Perhaps a card with a poem on about the size of a postcard would stick in their minds. Better still, why not a card three feet square? That wouldn't be mislaid or forgotten. Where can we get suitable card and how much will it cost?"

"I don't know, " said Princess Sticky.

"I know. I know," he cried as he leapt to his feet stamping ashes into a smoky cloud and with an excited flurry, darting like a startled rabbit, he ran from the kitchen into the field.

He returned in a matter of moments carrying the white enamelled side of an old gas oven. This he clattered on the floor and gleefully washed. And then Princess Sticky neatly printed one of his recently written pieces on the gleaming surface.

"This is Page One of The Tin Book," he declared.

"With these shields we will advance, surprise falsehood and confound duplicity.

The Magic Finger had pulled out and pointing shown the way. The Tin Book had happened.

The following Saturday was clear-skied, bright and dazzling, and Cinderfella and Princess Sticky taking with them Page One of The Tin Book, set off for the nearby village of Nobody Cares. Like good children skipping and laughing they bounced on the countryside, hopped stiles, ran under bridges, crossed streams, dodged through shady glades and on to the hard, regular lanes leading straight to the square in the centre of the village.

There they picnicked sharing the dandelion sandwiches which Princess Sticky had prepared beforehand.

As they ate, some little distance away, The Tin Book, passively leaning against a bench, faced the world for the first time. The shield was on station. In black and white the unacceptable face of art was at the hub of the shindig for all and sundry to read.

Cinderfella watching was soon totally engrossed with the reactions of the villagers as they moved around.
He wrote later:

> I watched the spasmic tinglings of nerve tissue, the fear, the embarrassment as passers moderated their pace from a casual stroll to an erratic hesitant stumble, as no longer looking where their feet were taking them they approached the brazen page with the dithering uncertainty of a non- expert rushing to defuse an IRA booby bomb. Then, wide-eyed they saw the big name. That did it. They visibly recoiled and the other wording hit their brains as a retinal blur, for almost involuntarily their heads jolted round and they marched on, goose pimples shuddering and feeling all over a letter-box crimson.
>
> What would the circle think if they were actually seen reading That….that…..that. Was he not……? Did he not……? Had he not…..? There was no doubt he had been seen picking cigarette ends up in the street that very day. That the words of such like gutter articles were entering their minds was unthinkable. Just too much. However one man's interest separated him from the rest.

Cinderfella spoke with him and soon learned the gentleman knew what he liked and liked what he saw for after a short pleasant chat he agreed to display pages of The Tin Book in a busy, highly respectable place in the village.

So overwhelmed was Cinderfella with this kindness, this show of confidence, this spontaneous goodwill that his gratitude was inexpressible.

Cinderfella and Princess Sticky, elated, soared homewards absolutely radiant, beaming warm gladness matching the sunshine of the day.

Magic finger stirrings were doing wonders.

Cinderfella and Princess Sticky vigorously worked and worked and worked producing and finding sites for more and more Tin Book pages. Soon they had taken them as far as their little legs would carry them.

Having reached this limit, Cinderfella hoped that others would take pages further afield but the close at hand acquaintance's network enmeshed rather than liberated and it quickly became clear that ugly brothers could not be relied upon to co-operate by performing this service. Consequently, Cinderfella realised he must have his own motor transport to dash about this brand new hot iron. Some ambition for a man with an empty pocket but let downs could not be allowed to interrupt the upsurge, the flow, the momentum, the vitality of this spirited advance.

At this moment, as if even lack of money could not be permitted to take industrious, novel enterprise and cast it aside, Magic Finger suddenly whisked up a wonderful decorated coach extraordinarily proper to the whole purpose, and another important link to its place in The Tin Book chain of good fortune.

A dilapidated sloppy old jalopy ice cream van that had stood idle, peacefully deteriorating for nearly two years. It was standing askew, behind a house, tyres flat, engine broken down, lights needing repair, chimes unworkable and the main body being used as a back garden shed, a junk store house of boxes, bags, jam jars, paint pots, wood, bits and bats filling the lower half of the back end.

It was a week's work for Cinderfella and Princess Sticky to couple up the horses, clear out the rubbish and clean the coach inside and out. Then one very wet Sunday afternoon they set off with the special container in the back full of delicious edibles to help them along the road and Tin Books in the windows providing everyone with food for thought.

They journeyed far and wide, over the hills and into towns and cities, often leaving behind the pages for the interested and the amazed to enjoy. Like greatness it was received all over and others now joined in the happiness of Cinderfella and Princess Sticky by carrying pages to places beyond the range of the decorated coach. Soon there were Tins in London and Liverpool and thickly clustered in many parts.

But 12 was struck come December and the wondrous lovely decorated carriage changed and all the goodies became bygones as if they'd been a happy dream, a phantom, an illusion. Cinderfella and Princess Sticky were plunged into misery and cold despair, sluggishly trudging through stinging winds and snow and The Tin Book went round slower and slower, every new page costing twenty times the energy of the first and no better for it. Cinderfella begged and friends helped a lot. Cinderfella and Princess Sticky were very grateful but knew their families had loads enough of their own. Then after smileless miles and miles came 'The Great Bear Trading Co-operative' and everyone intends to live happily ever after.

About the First Edition 1978

The 23rd of July '77 was a sunny afternoon and we were out in search of a site for Page Seventeen which I had just written and Blossom had just put on tin. So far we'd walked from Bell House to Mytholmroyd, Blossom had done some shopping and to help us decide the best place to make for we were having cups of tea in the Brass Lantern, a homely little café which is now a Chinese restaurant, when Janet Brown and Alan Bullock entered. I knew Janet. Not well, but to recognise. Bullock I had not met before. The four of us were the only customers in the place. They were, they told us, dashing around getting bits and pieces which would put the finishing touches to their new café, books and crafts complex in readiness for the first day of business on the coming Monday. Such news! Such news! We told them of our errand and nervously showed them the tin. Laughing, they simultaneously agreed to take the page for display at their new premises, called 'The Bear' and situated in Water Street, Todmorden. From our point of view, it had been an unexpected, fortunate, jolly meeting. Absolutely typical of The Tin Book spontaneity.

It must have been a fortnight later that we visited The Bear to change the page. There it was, on the little stove in the corner of the café. Outstanding. Honoured. It's a funny felling but that's how it felt. I came out as I went in, yet bigger, more complete, surer.

We made a great effort to change the page regularly.

The next definite event came when two of the three proprietors, namely Janet and Alan Bullock, wearying a little, eager for change and wanting challenge, opted to make The Bear a co-operative and thereby get more people involved. This they did.

All the while Blossom and I had our hands full surviving and changing tin pages.

'We would like to publish The Tin Book,' Alan Bullock said one day as suddenly as that; survival took all our stamina: as I'd just taken the weight off my legs in the café.

'Great,' I said. 'I'll get the manuscript to you as soon as possible.' And off we toddles.

In practice, as soon as possible was about a month and I placed the typescript with the Great Bear Trading Co-operative in April '78 when they said,

'We'll have it ready for sale in August.'

The next part, the long tale of lies, tricks and broken promises is as boring as an attack of hiccups.

Middle of August: 'Early September.'

Corruption is gaining the confidence of another and then avoidably being unworthy of that confidence.

Middle of September: 'Beginning of October.'

His poems will be first

A CRAGG VALE writer and regular contributor to The Hebden Bridge Times, Mr. G. W. Hoyles, will be the first person to take advantage of council backed publishing facilities in the Calder Valley.

A collection of poems by Mr. Hoyle, of Bell House Farm will be released through The Bear's Community book shop in Water Street, Todmorden. The shop opened recently with the aid of a £2,700 grant from the National Arts Council and is one of the first in the region to receive national backing. Its main aim is to make available books of high artistic and literary quality, which are normally only sold through outlets in larger towns. The organisers are also keen to hear from local writers who are interested in contributing to an anthology of creative art to be published and distributed through the bookshop. The Arts Council grant is to be used to provide fittings, fixtures and office equipment in the shop which is situated in Water Street. 'The Bear', as the shop is called, also aims to help local writers by providing an outlet for their work. Mr. Michael Dawson, Director of the Yorkshire Arts Council, through which the grant has been distributed, said this was one of the first community bookshops in the region to receive national backing. 'We have to be satisfied that the shop is set up and run on a non-profit making basis and has a charitable constitution,' said Mr. Dawson. He added that the grant had not to be used to provide stock for the shop but would go some way to help with the cost of the buildings conversion.

Clipping from front page local weekly 22nd September 1978

Worthwhile

In case any of your readers did not read beyond the first two paragraphs of the September 22nd Article re 'His poems will be first' I would like to draw attention to the worthwhile project of a few young people who have got together to meet a need in the area to provide books of all kinds.

They have been working for months now to open a café and bookshop and to my personal knowledge on little, or some weeks, no salary at all. These young people are hardworking and deserve all the support we can give them.

Mr. Hoyles poems no doubt are very clever - but to most of us a 'little way out' and if any of your readers have been 'put off' by this, may I suggest they visit The Bear bookshop in Todmorden.

I'm sure they will find their visit worthwhile.

Letters column 29th September 1978

"TIN BOOK" OFF PRESS

The first copies of a collection of poems entitled 'The Tin Book' by Cragg Vale writer, G.W. Hoyles, will be published later this month.

Mr. Hoyles, who lives at Bell House Farm, says the title is the obvious one for a collection of poems originally published on large pieces of metal which have been seen and read in many places.

'The publication will contain 100 of my poems and includes the controversial and conventional; pieces in the many styles around the poetic compass, even new nursery rhymes.'

'It is, I believe, a selection in which most people will find something they like and appreciate and is a poetry volume, the covers of which no one needs to be shy to look between. Indeed, one objective of the book is to make poetry a more generally read literary form,' said Mr. Hoyles. The book is being published by Bear Trading Co-operative of Todmorden and
is their first publishing venture.

Article 6th October 1978

End of November: 'Christmas.'

But The Tin Book was bound up and gagged in wrangle tangle.

After Christmas: 'In time for the exhibition.'

Traffic noise
Traffic noise
The throat clocks ticking traffic noise.

The exhibition came and went and then the café closed and the Great Bear began to dismember itself.

Bum.
Ignominious.

Look back: I was out and in, hung around a few hours. Heard the grumbles. Saw the sour faces; the scowls. I endured the tensions. I experienced something of the set up and I tend to think the Great Bear Trading Co-operative could be summed up as a gang of people ruefully doing jobs whilst battling for roles. Seeing each other , watching each other through work/ job status eyes. Thus the pettiest task assumes major importance. The most menial mundane job (the one everyone can do and no one will tackle) becomes the main nag; the biggest obstacle; the matter which must be cleared for success. They watched everything but that which they should have been watching, which was; the real accumulation of their expressed energy, the growth of their creation and the retention of that growth. Thus instead of revelling in each other's success, gaining satisfaction through expansion and making openings for others – that is the positive course of something long lasting – they competed with each other, fending off their personal frustrations by forcing others and each other to fail which is negative course to short lived orgasmic, ending with an astonished gasp.

Blame and counter blame.
Claim and counter claim
There's something in all of that bizarre.

The Tin Book had to be lodged securely in the memory of the printed page. And with the publishes shedding big chunks of empire; limbs falling off the grizzly, I felt obliged to step in and give them a hand to complete the book.

Enquiring, I was told all the printing had been done. Some was at a printers in Halifax. Some was at the Birchcliffe Centre, Hebden Bridge. Some was in a studio above the café. The big problem, so I was told, was the transport to collect the materials and take them to the binders.

The next morning, Blossom went to Halifax on the bus and collected all the printing there (3 reams A4 size. Big problem?) whilst I borrowed transport. We met in Hebden Bridge and called upon a Bear Co-operative member who was not at home in spite of prior arrangement, so the two of us went to Birchcliffe.

Page Seventeen.

Don't twist yourself.
To solve the riddle,
ask who's got
the biggest diddle.

G.W.Hoyles

Page Four.

And in the beginning was the word. And there came the conjunction and the word begat a word that begat a word till there was a book. And nouns mattered and verbs and adjectives. And sitting in rooms reading, the reading book begat a book which begat a book which begat a book which begat a book which begat a book and reading books are breeding reading books and profusion has brought confusion as message meaning is obscured.

Nouns are still. But theadjective has become everything as waiting they watch someone else translate the hard verbs.

They spend themselves on small fight and many are pointing the way shouting help whilst protecting the problems against solution.

G.W.Hoyles

Page Sixty One.

SUMS

ZM/03/05/86/D
R671987
\+

ONE MAN

G.W.Hoyles.

Through the good grace and courtesy

of the

City of Manchester Cultural Services,

The Tin Book

by

G.W. Hoyles

is available to the reading public

at the

Precinct Centre Library,

Precinct Centre, Oxford Road, Manchester

from the 5th to the 23rd of February 1979

between the times Ten a.m. and Nine p.m.

Monday to Friday only.

The Tin Book material was stacked along the wall of the open bay which houses the printing and duplicating equipment. Investigating this we were dismayed to find a fair amount still to be done and amazed to find well used plates but no corresponding printing.

Angry and suspicious I returned to the house where the Bear Co-operative member was living. This time he was at home and together we went to Birchcliffe.

We moved the printing there was to the house and after discussion it was accepted that I would take charge and do the work myself.

The same day I made arrangements with a printer, purchased from him ten plates and got an understanding that I could use the electric typewriter bought with arts money and kept in the office of the Bear Bookshop, Todmorden.

In Todmorden on the next day, Saturday, I collected from the studio above the café, Tin Book covers, end papers, the typescripts I'd given them a year before, photographs and everything I could find relevant to the book. I went to the bookshop and was told the typewriter was at a Whole Food shop by the market. We went there and started the job. Proceeding, it became clear that we would not finish the work in one sitting and after phoning the co-operative member for approval, arranged to take the typewriter to his home where we could work continuously until the typing was complete.

The plates and paste ups to print 37 pages of The Tin Book were delivered to the printer by Friday. And this, first paper edition of The Tin Book is the end product by my commando style salvage job.

G. W. Hoyles, Bell House Farm, Cragg Vale, Mytholmroyd, 6th April '79

ABOUT THE AUTHOR

Born 18th July 1936, Garstang, Lancashire.
Embarrassing bastard boy and only child of
Sarah Ellen Hoyles, a long suffering,
hardworking, nervous, ferocious, good hearted soul.
John Walmsey a Fleetwood Jeweller paid
7/6 a week towards my rearing.
My childhood years were a lonely, uneasy,
thought provoking time.
Went as new plasticine to the state run
plastic doll works for moulding.
But the Personnel were unsuccessful
I was not educated, I found out.

I've gone through the troubles. It has been
a rough, tortured life thus far.

G.W. Hoyles
March 1978

INDEX OF FIRST LINES

57100736R00073

Made in the USA
Charleston, SC
06 June 2016